Contents

Up and beyond!

It suddenly struck me that that tiny pea, pretty and blue, was the Earth. I put up my thumb and shut one eye, and my thumb blotted out the planet Earth. I didn't feel like a giant. I felt very, very small.

Neil Armstrong

Every 365 days, our planet Earth does a complete lap of a star we call the Sun. We don't often think of our Sun as one of the millions of stars in the sky. For most of us, it's just the Sun – a bright, hot ball that brings us light and warmth each day.

Not only is the Sun a star, it's also the centre of a vast system of moving planets. **Gravity** from the Sun holds Earth at just the right distance away so that we don't get too hot or cold. It also keeps the other planets spinning around it in their own unique **orbits**, which is why the planets don't collide.

Did you know?
It isn't just planets that move in orbits. Many of the planets have their own moons moving around them too. Jupiter has the most moons – 63 have been discovered so far!

LET'S FIND OUT

- What is meant by the term 'solar system'?
- How do the planets in our solar system stay in motion around the Sun?
- What kinds of planets are in our solar system?
- Where can humans go to experience the weightless conditions of space?
- What is it like to live and work on a space station?

gravity the force of attraction between two objects
orbits when an object in space moves around another on a regular path

The eight planets in our solar system orbiting the Sun

Our solar system

The solar system is the name we give to our Sun and the planets that move around it. It also includes smaller objects, such as moons, comets and **asteroids**.

The planets travel around the Sun on their own regular paths. These paths are called 'orbits'. The pull of gravity from the Sun keeps the planets in their orbits. It stops them from zooming off into space.

Our home

Of the eight planets in our solar system, Earth is the third from the Sun. It is about 150 million kilometres away from the Sun. This distance varies due to the shape of the Earth's orbit. Earth's orbit is **elliptical**, like a slightly flattened circle. So, sometimes the Earth is closer to the Sun than at other times.

Earth's neighbours

Neptune is the furthest planet from the Sun. It is 4.5 billion kilometres away from the Sun. Mercury is the closest. It is 58 million kilometres away from the Sun.

The four planets closest to the Sun are much smaller than the four outer planets. They are also made of very different substances. The four inner planets are mostly made up of rock and metal. The outer planets are mostly made up of gases and frozen liquids.

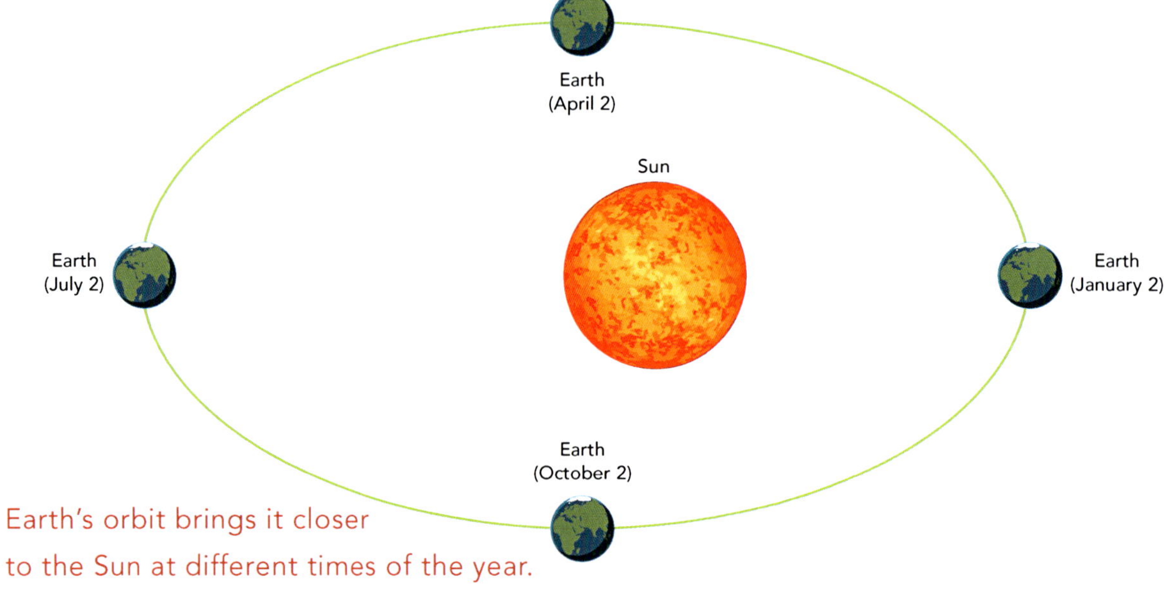

Earth's orbit brings it closer to the Sun at different times of the year.

asteroids small bodies or rocks orbiting the Sun
elliptical oval-shaped

It's hard to imagine just how big our solar system really is. If you drove a car non-stop at 100 kilometres an hour, it would take about 171 years to reach the Sun from Earth. At the same speed, it would take about 5000 years to drive to Neptune!

Models and diagrams give us a good idea of how the planets compare to each other in size. However, they don't give any idea of the distances between the planets and the Sun. On an accurate **scale diagram**, if Earth were the size of a pea, Jupiter would be 300 metres away. Neptune would be 1.5 kilometres from the pea!

The solar system is very well located. It is a part of the Milky Way galaxy, a huge spiral of about 200 billion stars. Our solar system is in one of the galaxy's outer arms, where there aren't too many stars crowded together. This is a good thing, because gravity from other stars could cause more comets to fly towards Earth. In this part of the galaxy, there is also much less **radiation** that could harm plants and animals.

Our solar system is a great place to call home!

The position of the eight planets in our solar system

scale diagram a diagram that accurately shows the size of one thing in relation to another

radiation rays or waves of energy that you cannot see

Breakaway tasks

Remembering

1 List the planets in our solar system.

2 How long would it take to drive to Neptune from Earth if you drove at 100 kilometres an hour?

Understanding

3 Using the diagram on page 5, write the order of the planets, starting with the planet closest to the Sun: Mars, Jupiter, Earth, Uranus, Saturn, Neptune, Venus, Mercury.

4 From information in the text, make up a facts quiz about the solar system with five questions. Swap your quiz with a classmate's.

Applying

5 Write some instructions to a person planning to drive their car to the Sun. Tell them how long it is likely to take, and suggest items they might need.

6 Put the most interesting facts from the report to the tune of a well-known song. Sing your solar system song to your classmates.

Analysing

7 Research and write a short biography of a famous scientist who discovered one of the planets in the solar system.

8 Use the Internet to research the Sun. Write a report that includes details about its size and its surface temperature.

Evaluating

9 Imagine that people wanted to move our solar system to another part of the galaxy. What would be your strongest argument for leaving it where it is?

Creating

10 Design a vehicle that could be used to explore the solar system. Think of ways to make it comfortable for long journeys, and recommend clean sources of energy to keep it moving.

Vote for me!

It's time to elect a new President of the Solar System. Who is the most suitable candidate? You decide!

Mercury

I'm Mercury, and I'm hot stuff! I'm the closest planet to the Sun, with a daytime temperature of more than 400 degrees Celsius. I'm rugged, too, covered with rocks and craters. I'm tough enough to be the best President of the Solar System ever!

Venus

I'm Venus, and there isn't much I can't offer. I've got raging volcanoes and craters all over my **molten** surface. My thick clouds lock in the Sun's heat and pour down **acid rain**. Forget Mercury – I'm the hottest planet of all. My daytime temperature is around 500 degrees Celsius!

Earth

I'm Earth. I'm the only planet in the solar system that supports life, which makes me the friendliest. I'm the perfect distance from the Sun – I don't get too hot or too cold. I even have an **atmosphere** that gives plants and animals protection from the Sun's rays.

Mars

I'm Mars. They call me the red planet, but there's more to me than red dust and rocks. I've got volcanoes and ice caps, and my surface constantly changes due to dust storms. But I always keep a cool head, because my thin atmosphere doesn't capture the Sun's heat.

molten in a melted form because of heat
acid rain rain that contains high levels of acidic chemicals
atmosphere a large pocket of gases surrounding a planet

Jupiter

I'm Jupiter. I'm the biggest planet in the solar system – 1300 times bigger than Earth. I have a rocky core, surrounded by an ocean of liquid **hydrogen**. I'm mostly made of poisonous gas, so no one will mess with me! I have a big red spot, too – it's a huge hurricane that's been raging for more than 300 years!

Saturn

I'm Saturn. With my system of rings, I'm surely the prettiest planet in the solar system. Like Jupiter, I'm huge and I have a rocky core, surrounded by gas. I'm a stormy planet, but my beautiful rings make up for it. They're made up of ice crystals, some as big as houses!

Uranus

I'm Uranus. No one knows much about me, so you can trust me to keep a secret! People think I have a rocky core, surrounded by water and other chemicals. I have rings too. They're thinner than Saturn's, but just as beautiful. My **methane** gas gives me my famous blue-green colour.

Neptune

I'm Neptune. My insides are made of rock and ice. I'm a deep blue colour thanks to the methane in my atmosphere. I have the wildest weather in the solar system. I'm also the furthest planet from the Sun. From out here, I can keep a close eye on the whole solar system!

hydrogen a gas, with no smell or colour, which is flammable (likely to catch alight)

methane a gas that makes up most of the natural gas we use in our homes

Breakaway tasks

Remembering

1 Which planet is the closest to the Sun?

2 Which planet is the biggest in the solar system?

Understanding

3 What do Saturn and Uranus have in common, and how are they different? Draw a Venn diagram to show their similarities and differences.

4 Make a summary list of the three most striking characteristics of each planet.

Applying

5 Write a 50–100 word 'letter to the editor' of a newspaper, explaining why Earth would be a good President of the Solar System.

6 Choose a planet. Find another three features that you could add to its campaign speech. Present the key points from your speech as a persuasive poster.

Analysing

7 Make a list of all the claims the planets make about their personalities or abilities rather than their physical characteristics.

8 List five questions you would ask each planet if you were writing a magazine article about them.

Evaluating

9 Of the eight planets in the article, which do you think makes the most convincing case to be elected president? Why?

Creating

10 Imagine that our Moon wants to be considered in the election for President of the Solar System. Research some interesting facts about the Moon and write a campaign speech for the Moon, similar to the speeches in the text. Present your speech to your class.

Life in orbit

Of all the places to work, a space station would have to be one of the most interesting. The International Space Station (ISS) has been in orbit around Earth since 1998. It circles Earth at a height of about 380 kilometres, in a similar way to how Earth orbits the Sun. It is as big as a five-bedroom house.

Most astronauts on the ISS stay no longer than six months. Others visit for shorter periods – sometimes no longer than two weeks.

The International Space Station (ISS)

Starting the day

The astronauts' day starts with the same routines as our days on Earth, but with a few extra challenges. Running water can't be used because it would float all over the station. Instead of taking baths or showers, astronauts wash with pre-packaged damp towels. To wash their hair they use a special shampoo that doesn't need to be rinsed out.

Working

The ISS is a floating **laboratory**. One of the astronauts' jobs is to study the effects of weightlessness on their bodies. They can see how people would cope with long space journeys, for example on possible future missions to Mars.

Keeping fit

Exercise is an important part of the crew's daily routine.

An astronaut exercising on the ISS

laboratory a room or building used for scientific research

Muscles and bones quickly weaken in the weightless environment of space.

Astronauts exercise for about two hours each day on specially designed equipment such as weights systems and treadmills.

Mealtimes

Astronauts' food is often supplied in **disposable** packages in a dried form. Water needs to be added to this type of food. Astronauts occasionally receive fresh food from visiting spacecraft, too. Salt and pepper have to be added to food in liquid form, so they don't float away and cause damage to equipment.

Playtime

The astronauts need time to relax as well. They can watch films, play games and listen to music. They can also talk to their families back on Earth. And they all enjoy looking out of windows at our beautiful planet below.

Bedtime

Astronauts can't sleep in normal beds, as they would simply float out of bed while they slept. They usually sleep in sleeping bags in small cabins. The bags are tied down so they don't move around too much.

Sleep is arranged by the clock and the shutters are closed, as there is no regular night time in space. The astronauts see the Sun set 16 times each day! At the end of their sleep time, they are woken by music, chosen for them by loved ones or **colleagues** back on Earth.

An astronaut ready for bed on the ISS

disposable something that is used once and then thrown away

colleagues people who work together or in the same field

Breakaway tasks

Remembering

1 How long has the International Space Station been in orbit?

2 What happens to muscles and bones in the weightless environment of space?

Understanding

3 Write five statements for a True/False quiz. Swap your quiz with a classmate's.

4 Using the information in the text, draw a picture of an astronaut preparing and eating breakfast.

Applying

5 Design a brochure to convince your classmates to take their next holiday on the International Space Station. Focus on space station experiences that are not possible on Earth.

6 Make a Pros and Cons chart about living for an extended time on the International Space Station.

Analysing

7 Make a list of personality traits that would be essential for a person spending a long period on the space station.

Evaluating

8 It costs the governments of many countries a lot of money to keep the International Space Station going. Write a paragraph about whether or not you think this is money well spent.

9 Imagine you are applying to work on the space station. Write a list of your experiences and personality traits that would be valuable to the crew.

Creating

10 Design your own space station and make a cardboard model of it. Include all the necessities mentioned in the article, and add special areas for other activities you would like to see the station used for.

George's Cosmic Treasure Hunt

Narrative

George's Cosmic Treasure Hunt is a book by Lucy and Stephen Hawking. In this extract, George is preparing for take-off.

The countdown is on! Nervously, George sits in his shuttle seat and waits for take-off …

Goodbye, Earth, thought George. *I'll be back soon*. He felt a twinge of sadness at leaving his beautiful planet, his friends, and his family behind. In just a short time he would be orbiting over their heads when the shuttle docked with the International Space Station. He would be able to look down and see the Earth as the ISS whizzed overhead, completing a full orbit once every ninety minutes. From space, he would be able to see the outlines of continents, oceans, deserts, forests and lakes, and the lights of big cities at night. Looking up from Earth, his mum and dad and his friends – Eric, Annie and Susan – would only see him as a tiny bright dot moving fast across the sky on a clear night.

"T minus thirty-one seconds. Ground launcher sequence go for auto sequence."

The astronauts wriggled slightly in their seats, wanting to get comfortable before their long journey. It felt surprisingly small and cramped inside the **cockpit**. Just getting into position for take-off had been a squeeze, and George had needed the help of a space engineer to clamber into his seat. The space shuttle stood upright for lift-off, so everything in the cockpit seemed as though it had been turned upside down. The seat was tilted back so that George's wasn't yet moving. He heard launch control again through his headset.

cockpit part of plane or rocket where the pilot sits

"We are go for launch at T minus five seconds and counting. Five, four, three, two, one. You are go for launch."

"Yes," said George very calmly, although inside he was screaming. "We are go for launch."

"T minus zero. Solid rocket booster **ignition***."*

The shaking increased. The two rocket boosters ignited underneath George and the other astronauts. It was like being kicked sharply in the backside. With a huge roar, the rockets broke through the silence, **propelling** the space shuttle off the launchpad and up into the skies. George felt as though he had blasted off from Earth while strapped to an enormous firework. Anything could happen now – it could explode, it could **veer** off course and crash back to Earth, or head up into the skies and spin out of control. And there would be nothing George could do about it.

Through the window, he saw the blue of the Earth's atmosphere all around the spaceship, but he could no longer see the Earth itself. He was leaving his own planet!

ignition being ignited (set on fire)
propelling pushing forcefully
veer turn sharply

Breakaway tasks

Remembering

1. Where does George hope his shuttle will soon be docking?
2. Who helped George to clamber into his seat?

Understanding

3. Find two sentences in the story that show George's feelings as he prepares for take-off.
4. Number these events in the order in which they occur in the story:
   - George sees the blue of the Earth's atmosphere all around the spaceship.
   - The two rocket boosters ignite.
   - George feels a twinge of sadness about leaving Earth.
   - The astronauts wriggle in their seats to get comfortable.

Applying

5. Imagine you are a crew member on George's mission. Write a log, recording the major events leading up to the take-off.
6. Use the Internet to find information about a recent space rocket launch. Make a launch profile poster, including information about the time and date of the launch, where the launch took place and what its mission was.

Analysing

7. Make a list of the personality traits you think would be important to have as an astronaut. Put a tick beside the traits that George seems to possess.
8. Describe how George might feel when his shuttle manages to dock safely at the International Space Station.

Evaluating

9. Do you think children should be allowed to take part in real-life space missions? If so, what special attributes do you think children could bring to a space mission?

Creating

10. Design a new type of spaceship that George could take to the space station. Design it to make the journey as fun as possible, as well as safe. Showcase your design on a colourful poster or make a model of it.

Strands in action

Core tasks

1 Design and name your own solar system. On poster paper, draw a star and a range of planets surrounding it. Write a fact file about the planets in your solar system, naming each planet and listing their special features. At least one of them should have features that would support life.

2 Record an advertisement to encourage people from Earth to visit your new solar system. Come up with a catchy jingle listing the features of each planet to attract people. Make sure that at least one of your planets can offer fun activities.

Extra tasks

1 Make a crossword puzzle using the names of the planets in our solar system, and any other space words you've come across in this magazine. Give a short, clear clue for each word.

2 Make a graph of the amount of time you think an astronaut on the International Space Station spends on their daily tasks, for example, exercising, working and eating.

3 What kinds of music do you think the people on the International Space Station would listen to at different times of the day? Make a playlist for a day on the space station.

4 Research and write a short report on another object that orbits Earth, such as a satellite or a piece of space junk.

In your own writing, remember the difference between 'it's' (short for 'it is') and 'its', which refers to ownership of something ('the dog wagged its tail').

Remember the difference between 'they're' (short for 'they are'), 'their', which indicates ownership, and 'there', which indicates place.